Elfi Schöniger

The Legend of Conner MacSheep

About this book:
With an ironic wink "The Legend of Conner MacSheep" tells the story of a sheep with a very human personality and his flock in the Scottish Highlands. Despite a sinister omen that overshadows his birth, he has a joyful childhood. As a teenager he proves himself at the annual Highland Sheep Games and falls in love.
But then the much-feared prophecy fulfills itself...

The story takes the reader into the miraculous world of the Scottish Highlands with its traditions, legends and adorable animal and human inhabitants. It will appeal to teenagers and adults who like it tense but also humorous.

Author/Illustrator
Elfi Schöniger, born in 1955, lives and works in the same hilly Taunus region of Germany that inspired the Grimm brothers to collect and record local folk and fairy tales. She and her husband have an adult daughter.
Inspired by her family, surroundings and travels, Elfi wrote her first children's story in 1994. She personally creates the illustrations in most of her books.

Translator
Andrew Catford is a native of Perth, Scotland, and attended his first Royal Highland Gathering in Braemar at the age of five. He is intimately familiar with the glens and mountains of the Grampians.
Andrew now lives and works in Colorado, within easy reach of the High Rockies, but also returns regularly to Scotland and his beloved Grampian Mountains.

The Original "Die Legende von Conner MacSheep"
was published by Edition Schöne Bücher, 2009,
ISBN: 9783940712110
Copyright © Elfi Schöniger

Elfi Schöniger

The Legend of Conner MacSheep

Real Highlanders wear wool!

Translated from the German
by
Andrew Catford

BoD

Originally published in Germany in 2009
as *Die Legende von Conner MacSheep*
by Edition Schöne Bücher, Gemünden, Germany

Copyright 2009 © by Elfi Schöniger
Translation copyright 2014 © by Andrew Catford

All rights reserved.

Book Design by Elfi Schöniger
Cover Design by Elfi Schöniger
Illustrations by Elfi Schöniger

Publisher: BoD – Books on Demand, Norderstedt, Germany

ISBN: 9783735757081

Bibliograf.Information der Deutschen Nationalbibliothek:

Die Deutsche Nationalbibliothek verzeichnet diese Publikation in der Deutschen Nationalbibliografie, detaillierte Bibliografische Daten sind im Internet über
http://dnb.dnb.de abrufbar.

Dear Reader,

The legend told in this book has its origins in my imagination. The names of the Scottish towns and scenes are real. But I have adapted them geographically to the story, placed imaginary buildings in them and populated them with entirely fictitious humans and animals.

Nevertheless, every one of the places mentioned rewards personal exploration. And you will find the real inhabitants every bit as enjoyable as my inventions.

Fàilté - Welcome to Scotland.

Yours,

Elfi Schöniger

PS: Somewhere I read that, according to ancient lore, Scottish sheep are said to have the gift of speech, because their bones were used in prehistoric times to foretell the future and their skin was used to make the bag for that remarkable instrument, the Great Highland Bagpipe. So ...

When the days of heroes, sagas and legends were already far in the past, when the mystical had been ousted by reason and technology and mankind slogged through the daily grind of work, household chores, home and sleep, *he* was born.

The Beginning

Dark gray clouds covered most of the evening sky. Only here and there did a star twinkle. It was cold, with no sign of spring. The wind whistled through every cranny in the fold. All of the sheep stood, huddled together, and eyed the new member of the flock. Caitlin, the new mother, licked and caressed her baby lamb. Gently nuzzling him with her nose, she urged him to stand up. The onlookers gave their support with friendly bleats.

Finally he succeeded. He stood there with legs spread. The cold made him shiver, but a tiny flame of curiosity and zest for life already flickered in his eyes. Raising his head, he announced his presence in this world with a resounding "baah." Then he sought and found his very own source of food and devoted himself to it with abandon.

"Congratulations, Caitlin! What a cute little lamb! And so strong!" came the loud praise from the onlookers. Unkind speculation about the father was murmured less openly. Olivia, a spinster sheep, dedicated herself to the malicious gossip with special intensity.

"Did you see his wool? And how his eyes glow?" she whispered to her sister. Ellie nodded deliberately. She could not answer. Her mouth was too full. More than anything, she loved to eat.

Olivia assumed her I-KNOW-FOR-A-FACT expression and prophesied: "That one's definitely going to cause a lot of trouble." And continued, with a pitying gaze, "Poooor Caitlin!"

Ellie nodded again and continued to chew contentedly. Since no other sensible response could be expected from her sister, Olivia turned to Janet. "A lamb with green eyes and curls. That's completely unacceptable!"

Normally disregarded, Janet was visibly pleased with the attention and, seeking approval, added, "There's a full moon tonight!"

Olivia immediately recognized this as a further omen and predicted spitefully,

"Born by the light of a full moon

– trouble is sure to follow soon!"

Ellie dropped the hay from her mouth in horror. "Are you saying this lamb isn't a lamb? What else could it be?"

Sudden silence. All of the sheep stared at her. Olivia drew up her skinny body under their questioning gaze and brusquely said, "Everyone knows that! Anything is possible when the moon is full." She lifted her head and looked around challengingly.

"And just what might this *anything* be?" asked Caitlin pugnaciously, with voice raised.

"I don't want to talk about it," Olivia replied sharply, "But I know what I know," she concluded and turned away.

"Yes, and I know that you know absolutely nothing," Caitlin answered defiantly, but her eyes filled with tears. "What a miserable goat," she thought. That old maid was simply jealous. She turned to her lamb and lovingly licked his small head."Let them talk. I love both you and your father. One day you'll be just as strong and brave as he is. Then they'll look up to you and the evil gossip will vanish into thin air," Caitlin whispered. For a moment she daydreamed, then sighed a deep sigh. With shining eyes, she looked on her little lamb and said solemnly, "You shall bear his name. Conner! Conner MacSheep of Clan MacSheep. A name you can be proud of."

But Conner was not yet interested in fame and glory. He was already asleep, fed and content in the silvery light of the full moon. The remainder of the flock had settled down long before. In any case, most of them remained aloof when there were quarrels. To get involved in something you would rather not know about was simply stupid. That is why they were more than ready to immediately forget what they had heard.

Conner's Childhood

Conner only had four needs in the days and weeks that followed: feeding, sleeping, frolicking and finding answers. In other words: He bombarded every sheep in the flock with questions. They rang from morning until evening: "Why does the sun only shine during the day? Why does heather taste so bitter? Why can't sheep fly? Why does gorse make my nose yellow? Can you sleep while standing? Where does the wind come from? Why are there no green sheep? Is it possible to ...?" While gazing innocently at his victim.

He always listened attentively. Some answers made his eyes sparkle, others called for more questions. Many members of the flock willingly gave detailed information, although some were less generous.

Whichever way you look at it, everyone was happy to see Conner, despite his enormous curiosity. The initial whispering faded and it would remain that way as long as nothing out of the ordinary happened. Indeed, many a sheep left a tasty tuft of herbs standing for him.

Conner thrived splendidly.

One beautiful day in early summer, Adam the shepherd set off with the flock to another pasture. "We are going on vacation to Fairy Glen," sighed Ellie with delight and rolled her eyes. Her mental movie theater promised lush pastures, abundant space, peace and quiet.

"Yes, yes," said Olivia. She plucked at a gorse bush and rolled her head meaningfully. "The thing is, it is really lonely there, especially at night."

Ellie hesitated. "But that is the very best part. No shepherd, no dogs, spend the whole day ea.., er..., hmm, doing whatever we want."

"Eating! Just say it! It's the one thing that interests you."

"Oh, come on, Olivia. What is making you so gloomy?" Ellie asked sweetly.

"I can not tell you now," Olivia said grandly. "But the danger is not over. On the contrary. It grows with each passing day – and it will strike suddenly, when it is least expected. I, however, can still remember his father and grandfather. And I would not care to meet either of them by the light of the moon. Even though you are all infatuated with Conner, I am going to remain alert."

And to prove her thoroughness, she immediately checked with a glance to her rear, where she presumed Conner would be. In doing so, she unfortunately failed to see a rock in her path and landed on her thinly padded bottom. Ellie had seen it coming. As sorry as she felt for the groaning Olivia, she giggled mischievously. Olivia gave her an insulted look and trudged off.

Meanwhile, Conner could hardly contain his curiosity. "What is the Fairy Glen like? Is it a long walk? Is there a loch there? Are there lots of sheep? Will we have a byre[1] there or will we sleep outdoors?"

"My goodness! So many questions! I'm afraid you'll have to wait until we arrive," Caitlin laughed. Conner frisked around boisterously, bumping into several sheep.

"Oops, my lad. There is no need to go wild," Janet reprimanded him kindly.

"Sorry, Auntie Janet, but I'm so excited. I've never been away from here before. Mummy thinks I have to wait and see. But I can't!" Conner leaped around excitedly.

He'd said 'Auntie Janet.' A wave of joy swept over the elderly ewe. Blushing, she began to compose an educationally valuable answer, but Conner had already disappeared into the crowd. "Such a nice laddie," she thought. "Olivia must simply be wrong. But even if she is not? Surely the old curses eventually lose their power."

And off they set.

---

[1] Byre (Scottish) = A shed for farm animals.

Fairy Glen

The Fairy Glen was even more wonderful than Conner had imagined during the journey. Hills covered in deep green and purple were interspersed with boulders piled on and alongside each other and picturesque groves of birch trees. But the most beautiful part was the loch. The surface glistened mysteriously like a mirror of bronze and ruins of a castle stood on a promontory to the west. The most splendid meadow of flowers Conner had ever seen stretched as far as the eye could see. He was overwhelmed.

Conner walked in unusual silence behind his mother until evening. Only after they found a place to sleep next to a boulder did Conner speak again. "Have you been here before? Can you tell me anything about the castle and the loch, Mummy?" And added, with almost clairvoyant assurance, "Did Daddy like it here, too?"

Caitlin nodded.

"I met your father for the first time in this glen." She looked dreamily toward the loch. "We had already been here for several days when he suddenly appeared before me one evening. He showed me Dun Eagle[2], the castle ruin, and told me its history. We were inseparable in the days and weeks that followed. We explored the area and were very much in love. He was always happy and friendly. But then he vanished just as suddenly as he had popped up." Caitlin's voice became hoarse. "Then the others said that there was something not quite right about him. Some even claimed that he was under a curse. And all that merely because there was a full moon when he disappeared. What superstitious nonsense." After a while, she added, "But even if it were true, it doesn't change the fact that I still love him."

They spent the following days exploring the new pasture. Conner, especially, could not be held back. He felt like a great explorer and often did not return to the flock until darkness fell. His mother worried, because she did not want to recognize that, slowly but surely, Conner was growing up. Her child was a teenager now. And like every individual at this stage of development, he was more difficult and stubborn than before.

He certainly behaved strangely when Abbie was nearby. Abbie was Holly and Ross' youngest daughter and only two weeks older than Conner. Her eyes glowed like dark amber and her soft fleece gleamed like liquid honey in the sunlight.

---

[2] Dun (Gaelic) = Castle

If she came near Conner, he suddenly strutted instead of walking. He baahed and bleated as loud as a steam locomotive while his eyes flashed in challenge. Yet Abbie did not appear to notice him. She simply looked straight through him. If by chance she could not see Conner, she twisted her neck until she caught sight of him, only to immediately ignore him once more. The other sheep grinned and were reminded of their own youth.

So the weeks went by in blissful grazing and sleeping. Conner's flamboyant behavior became more subdued and Abbie rewarded him more frequently with friendly glances. Indeed, they even undertook forays together to unknown spots.

One day they discovered the entrance to a small side valley where the flowers bloomed even more luxuriantly than on their summer pasture. Red, yellow and blue flowers competed with various grasses for their attention.

"Just look, there are even flowers on the trees here," Abbie said in wonder.

Always looking for an opportunity to impress Abbie, Conner dashed off to gather the "tree flowers" for her. Standing on the very tips of his hind hooves, he stretched up toward the branches. The silver-colored bells gave off an enchanting aroma. He reached for the cluster of flowers with pursed lips and plucked it. The blossom nectar had barely moistened his tongue when a wave of craving and pleasant longing passed through him. He greedily gobbled down his prize. He felt how a strange tingling and pull spread from his belly to every nerve ending. Seconds later, the sensation was gone. To his amazement, he found that he had not saved a single blossom for Abbie. He shook himself and returned to her in confusion.

Abbie gazed into Conner's eyes and was spellbound. It was as if tiny sparks leaped out of them. They seemed to shine from inside. He had never looked at her in this way before. It was really eerie. So why, at the same time, was there such a pleasant tingling in the nape of her neck?

Later, neither of them knew how long they had stood speechless, facing each other. Conner was the first to break the silence. He took a deep breath and nudged Abbie with his nose. "Come on, let's go back. But this valley remains our secret. Promise?"

"Promise," Abbie said.

They both trotted back to the flock in silence. Something indefinable had changed between them. Independently they attempted to understand what could have set off this tingling in the belly, because the sensation could not be compared to anything they had experienced before. It was a little like peering into the depths from the cliffs by the loch. Equal parts fear and a pleasant shiver.

Jamie hopped toward them when they

reached the pasture. "Hurry up. Come with me! There will be a big party tonight," he chattered excitedly, "and the Highland Sheep Games take place again tomorrow. John McMullen has come with his people from the Grampian Mountains and Jack Cross and Cat Bluebell are here with their great Highland bagpipes and Dongdong has brought the bass drum."

"Wow, fantastic," Abbie cheered. "I'm allowed take part in the dancing this year and I might even win a prize. Mum told me that I'm really very good. What do you think?"

She looked questioningly at Conner. But Conner was bothered by other worries.

"Is Hamish with them?" he asked Jamie, who was still bouncing around.

"Aye!"

"And? Is he taking part?" Conner was slowly losing patience. "Great Sheep[3]! Jamie, don't force me to squeeze it out of you one word at a time!"

"Dad said that Hamish has become a real fighter." Jamie hemmed and hawed. "Although I don't understand why he now has so many parts from other animals."

"What do you mean by that?"

"Dad said: 'Just look at this guy. A head like an ox, and with that bull neck, he can cushion any header,' Jamie quoted. Abbie and Conner

---

[3] Great Sheep! = Oath, roughly equivalent to 'my goodness!'

almost burst with laughter.

"But Jamie, those are only comparisons. It simply means that he is very strong and can withstand a lot. Hamish is as much a sheep as ever," Abbie told him.

Jamie scraped awkwardly with his hooves. "But when you see him, you'll understand," he whined and hurried away from them.

"Poor Jamie," said Abbie.

"Nonsense! He has to put up with it or he'll never learn," Conner said. "But if Hamish actually has become so strong ... "

"You don't necessarily have to go up against him. In any case, he fights in another age group," Abbie said, trying logic.

Suddenly, Conner was furious. "That has nothing to do with it! He is mean and I'm going to show him that he's a nobody." Louder than necessary, he continued. "Girls just don't have a clue!" With a red face, he stomped off, leaving a stunned Abbie behind.

In the evening, all the sheep gathered around the campfire and celebrated their reunion. When Nathan MacAngus, the old clan chieftain, got up after some time, the talkative gathering fell silent. He cleared his throat and, for a moment, enjoyed the rapt attention. He then spoke in a clear, deep voice. "Once again I am delighted to be able to welcome a friendly flock to our Highland Sheep Games this year.

'Mile fàilte!'[4] to our friends – and tomorrow's opponents – from the Grampian Mountains."

–Restrained applause.–

"And even more sincere thanks for their contribution to our joint party tomorrow evening: a keg of Grandsheep's Best whisky."

–Tumultuous applause.–

With a friendly nod in the direction of the guests, Nathan continued. "Tomorrow's heavy events[5] for the rams are the jump for height[6], jump for distance[7] and press-o'-war[8]. The hill race, music and dance contests and the ever-popular pattern nibbling[9] are open to everyone. This evening, every contestant is granted an extra serving of salt and mineral lick. The Highland Sheep Games begin early tomorrow with a muster of registered participants directed by Ellie and Olivia, who will also show you the venues for your events. And now, I wish everyone a good night."

---

[4] Mile fàilte! (Gaelic) = A thousand welcomes!

[5] Heavy events = Highland games contests, often for professional contestants.

[6] Jump for height = High jump; in this case a special event for rams, explanation at the "venue".

[7] Jump for distance = Long jump; in this case a special event for rams, explanation at the "venue".

[8] Press-o'-war = Head butting; in this case a special event for rams, explanation at the "venue".

[9] Pattern nibbling = Very special event for ewes, explanation at the "venue".

HIGHLAND SHEEP GAMES

Shortly after sunrise, bustling activity already prevailed. Everyone wore their traditional kilts in honor of the games and their flock. Conner also wore his clan's tartan[10] for the first time. Abbie hopped like a ping-pong ball, supposedly to loosen her muscles. The elderly stood together and looked on benignly. Several thought wistfully of their own youth. Finally, Dongdong played a roll on the drum and Nathan MacAngus' voice rang across the field.

"Madainn mhath![11] I hereby declare this year's Highland Sheep Games open. I wish you every success. There is only one rule for participants. Play a fair game!"

After this starting signal, Ellie and Olivia were almost overwhelmed by excited participants. Ellie rose to the occasion with unexpected style. She organized, named venues and times, waved and wiggled her legs and, as a bonus, even had a smile ready for everyone. On the other hand, Olivia looked on very grouchily.

---

[10] Tartan = Woven plaid pattern in clan colors.
[11] Madainn mhath! (gaelic) = Good morning!

She would rather have gossiped in the background than worked in the foreground. But today she had to resign herself.

Conner had registered for every heavy event and the hill race. However, his contests were timed so he could see Abbie dance the Highland fling[12] during his lunch break. Abbie, though, had time before her auditions to cheer Conner on. Later, they would run the hill race together.

Jamie overtook them on the way to the loch shore where the jump for distance contest took place. He ran so fast that almost the only sign of him was a passing flash of color. His plaid[13] fluttered and his family's colors shone in the sun. The audience was already in place when the athletes arrived.

"To make everything fair for this year's participants, we have introduced a small preliminary test," Nathan said in his welcome. "Anyone who can leap across the Black Water River where it enters the loch qualifies for the jump for distance."

Quiet groaning and a reluctant clatter of hooves could be heard.

"Why does everyone need to be tested? It should be enough if the young sprouts show whether they can do it," Hamish said and

---

[12] Highland fling = Scottish dance in place with complicated sequence of steps.
[13] Plaid = Light tartan blanket worn over the shoulder.

adopted a stance with legs spread.

"You're afraid that you won't make it!" Conner and Ben called from the crowd. They looked at each other in astonishment and then laughed aloud.

"Great minds think alike," Nathan said and smiled at them.

The young rams grinned widely, took a run-up and leaped lightly over the stream. A genuine stampede followed. It was no longer possible to determine whether someone had simply been blocked in front of the opposite bank by the jam. The preliminary test could not be scored. Only one young ram was denied permission to join in. Jamie had attempted to slip through. But he had landed in the middle of the stream and now stood between the others, soaking wet. Nevertheless, he was very welcome as a mascot for Conner and Ben.

JUMP FOR DISTANCE

Nathan MacAngus strode to the center of the space to serve as umpire. The long jumpers took up positions in a semicircle behind the freshly mowed run-up track.

"Was it you who trimmed the track so neatly, Ellie?" asked Caitlin, who stood in the front row of the audience.

Ellie nodded proudly.

"Who else could have eaten so much at one time," Olivia said and rolled her eyes.

Ellie blushed, but did not defend herself.

The start signal rang out from the tower in the ruins. Ben was first to start. He bounced like a rubber ball, swinging his legs when he was airborne. Without warning, he began to run. He bounced three times on all four feet, leaped and landed on the sandy shore. Two assistants quickly verified and announced the distance. "Six poles."[14]

Applause rang out from the crowd.

Hamish came next. He bent his knees, lowered his chest and took a deep breath. For several seconds he resembled a bronze statue. Then he exhaled and ran. He leaped up before the marker, giving away precious ground, and landed so heavily on the loch shore that he almost somersaulted and then lay there.

Megan and Ross, who had first aid duty, were rushing toward the beach when Hamish suddenly stood up and shook himself.

"Seven and a half poles," called one of the assistants.

Hamish grinned broadly and ran to his

---

[14] Pole = ancient Sheep Games measurement; one pole is equal to the height of the chief's shoulder. Only full and half poles are counted.

people who greeted him with slaps on the back. Shaking their heads, Megan and Ross returned to their positions.

Now it was Conner's turn. He made three low hops and began to run. He hit the mark on takeoff and landed on all fours after a graceful flight.

The assistants measured with the staff. "Eight and a half poles for Conner MacSheep. The best jump, so far," one of the assistants called out excitedly.

Two high voices screamed above the roar of applause. Jamie and Abbie expressed their enthusiasm in loud shouts of "Conner! Conner!"

Then Ryan, Daniel and three Grampian flock athletes jumped, but no one surpassed the eight and a half poles turned in by Conner.

JUMP FOR HEIGHT

After a short breather for contestants and public, the next heavy event began. The jump for height contest demanded close attention from the umpires. A bundle of heather for each participant lay on the remains of the old castle wall. The goal was to kick the bundle down with a hoof. Heads could not be used. Contact with the wall was allowed, but it was advisable to avoid this if possible. The wall was certainly old, but literally hard as stone. Every contestant was given five opportunities to send the heather to the ground. The winner was whoever succeeded with the fewest attempts.

On the way to the venue, Ben and Conner met Hamish and his fans.

"Pushing flowers around isn't my thing," Hamish said pompously and gained approving hoots from his entourage. "I prefer to fortify myself for the press o' war, even though there really is no serious opponent," he added and turned off in the direction of the catering area.

"If I were as fat as you are, I'd avoid it too. You'd bring the wall down," Ben joked.

"Or everyone would think it was an earthquake, run away, and there would be no one there to admire him, " Conner scoffed.

"At least my fans have already left kindergarten," Hamish retorted as he moved on.

With shrugs, Conner and Ben turned and ran to the venue. When they reached the wall, they stared in amazement. It was at least four poles high and the heather bundles were twice as large as a sheep's head. Never mind 'pushing flowers around.' This required every ounce of jumping ability and accuracy. Ben looked questioningly at Conner.

"Wouldn't it be better to save our strength?

I'm afraid it's going to get even harder."

But Conner already had plans for the heather bundle that he had yet to win. He wanted to give it to Abbie. So he simply gave Ben a friendly push and nodded toward the starting point.

"Let's go," he said tersely and began to run.

A total of only six participants had registered for the jump for height: Conner, Ben, Ryan and three rams from the Grampian flock. The contestants started in alphabetic order. Ben came first.

He took a few small hops in place to built momentum. Then he leaped up. Unfortunately, not high enough. He flexed briefly and jumped a second time, again too low. However, the third attempt was successful. Literally flying upwards, he kicked the bundle of heather down in a wide arc. He was rewarded with cheers and loud applause.

Next came Carl from the Grampians. Carl was lightly built and seemed to have a rubber ball in every foot. At the first attempt, he catapulted higher than the wall and casually flicked the flowers down. Audience and contestants gave ungrudging applause.

Conner followed. He used the same technique as Ben. And he was successful with his third jump. Then came truly dull, unsuccessful attempts by the two guest entrants.

Now it was Ryan's turn. He jumped from a standing position, flew upwards and landed on his belly on top of the wall. The onlookers screamed. Ryan floundered with every foot in the air. The first aid team responded like lightning. With support from the contestants, they were able to free Ryan from this tricky situation.

When his hooves again touched solid ground, tumultuous applause broke out. Ryan bowed briefly before his audience, nodded to the rescuers and quickly disappeared behind the ruin. His girlfriend found him there with a bright red face and trembling knees.

After this dramatic event the onlookers and contestants moved on to the music and dance contests, which were dominated by ewes.

HIGHLAND FLING

To warm up, Abbie performed strange-looking stretching exercises with her hind legs. At intervals she tugged nervously at her kilt. Standing still had been a foreign concept to her for hours. It was no different for Kathie, Abbie's best friend. At one moment they were still stretching their hind legs with serious expressions and in the next moment they could hardly stay on their feet for laughing. Emma, the youngest member of the trio, watched everything with great interest, but did not understand. She was still too young for dancing and could not care less about rams. Nevertheless, she truly admired the graceful postures that her friends displayed and it was usually possible to get along with Conner and Ben. So, as a good friend, she also tolerated today's nonsense.

The dance contest venue was the castle courtyard. There was a natural stage for the participants and the audience could make themselves comfortable at or on the castle wall. The musicians used accompaniment of the dance contest as a warm-up for the musical competition.

"Dear friends," Nathan began. "It was a great pleasure to see how many young ewes wished to enter the Highland fling competition. Once again, I ask for understanding from all of those who are not yet nine months old. They can take part next year. I ask everyone else to come to the stage to draw a starting number. Those musicians who have volunteered as accompanists for the first round may now take their places on stage with their instruments."

A crowd of excited dancers immediately gathered in front of the stage. The musicians behind them saw no possibility of reaching the stage until Dongdong and Ross beat a drum roll. The dancers promptly cleared a wide path to the stage. Both drummers and three pipers took up their places in the background.

Nathan stepped onto the stage. "The competition will be decided by elimination. First, two ewes dance, competing against each other. The winners of this stage then dance in threes, each against the others. The winner bears the title 'Highland Fling Queen' until next year's Sheep Games." Smiling, Nathan cleared his throat. "I now invite the first pair, draw numbers one and two, up to the stage. Please give a big round of applause to welcome Kathie and Lucy."

The audience clapped enthusiastically. Both dancers hurried to their positions and assumed the initial stance. The applause stopped abruptly when Dongdong twirled the drumsticks above his head. Caitlin, Holly and Daniel moistened their lips and held their bagpipes ready.

The bass drum beat out a rhythm, and the snare drum and pipers joined in. Kathie and Lucy both tapped one more beat with the front hoof, straightened up and began the fast, complicated sequence of steps in the Highland fling. It took only a short time before the audience began to clap in time.

When the dance was over, the terraces erupted. Lucy and Kathie nervously watched the jury, consisting of Nathan, Olivia and John McMullen. "Two points for Lucy, one for Kathie", Nathan announced. Lucy was therefore in the final round.

"Ewes with starting numbers three and four to the stage, please," Nathan called over renewed applause for the first pair.

Lauren and her opponent from the Grampian Mountains took their positions. The drum began to beat again, the pipes joined in and the dancers tapped in time. They straightened up and danced. Lauren stared into the distance with a fixed gaze while her feet performed the complex steps. On the other hand, her opponent smiled at the audience and skipped lightly, as if it were child's play. So this round went to Niamh from the Grampian Mountains.

Then Abbie and Sarah stepped onto the stage. Their excitement was clearly visible. Abbie's gaze swept the audience until she picked out Conner. He nodded encouragingly to her and she smiled back bravely. Then it grew quiet and Abbie was sure that everyone could hear her heart beat. At the first drumbeat she gave a start, but she had already forgotten her surroundings when the snare drum and pipes joined in. Her feet moved unconsciously in time with the music that filled her head. She felt fantastic and could have kept on dancing for reel after reel. However, the music ended and Abbie was back on the stage. The bashfulness returned. She finally curtsied and stared at the floor. The jury deliberated, gesticulating vigorously. Suddenly, Olivia's voice shrilled,

"I should know. After all, I was Highland Fling Queen for five years in succession. Abbie certainly danced, but that was not a Highland fling. Put kindly, one might say that her steps were not in the correct sequence. She lost."

Nathan looked at John McMullen. He nodded in agreement and Nathan therefore announced, "The winner of the third set is Sarah. We shall see you again after a brief pause for refreshments."

Holly was waiting for Abbie at the stage exit. She said, "You danced beautifully, darling," and hugged Abbie. "Unfortunately, it really was not a Highland fling, but your dance was very expressive. Everyone was thrilled. Poor Sarah was completely rattled and missed the beat twice. That's why the decision was difficult for the jury and Nathan would rather have awarded the victory to you. However, Olivia is correct when she insists that the proper sequence of steps counts for more than graceful dancing. So don't be sad, sweetheart. In a way, you also won."

Abbie actually had no memory of what she had danced. She felt a little dazed, but accepted her mother's explanation. Conner stood in the background and overheard everything. "I think your dancing was terrific. You made it look so easy and you smiled the whole time. Olivia is an old nanny goat and simply jealous because she can no longer take part. You should have won," Conner said with feeling.

Then it simply happened. Without knowing how they started, real torrents flowed from Abbie's eyes. Her nose ran and her whole body trembled. Holly held her child tightly in her arms and stroked her back soothingly. Conner was not sure what he should do and placed his arm on Abbie's shoulder. It did not last long. Abbie raised her head, sniffed loudly once more and then laughed, making Holly and Conner's ears ring.

"So, now everything is fine again, " Abbie said with spirit. "I can't remember anything after the moment the music started. I'm sure the jury made the correct decision. And when you say I was good, I believe you."

She wiped her nose thoroughly and then announced, "I'm hungry and thirsty. Who is coming with me to the catering tent?"

After all three were refreshed, they returned to the stage to see the final decision. The excited participants were already in position. Sarah and Niamh had clearly flushed cheeks and ears while Lucy looked around rather casually. Nathan waved a prompt to the newly formed orchestra. Callum hit the bass drum. Ross added the snare drum. Cat Bluebell, Jack Cross and

Daniel joined in with their bagpipes. The dancers stood upright and kicked off. Sarah seemed rather tense. She lurched on the first turn and could only recover at the last moment. In the second and third turns her dancing was so energetic that only a brief break allowed her to get in time with the music again.

Lucy watched Sarah from the corner of her eye, which did not improve her dancing style. Although she made no errors, she also did not appear particularly enthusiastic.

Quite unlike Niamh. Her hooves hardly seemed to touch the floor. She pointed her legs gracefully to the side, hopped lightly in place, and spun with vigor, her forelegs flying through the air in elegant arcs. In a word, Niamh's dancing stole the hearts of the jury and everyone else. So it was an easy decision to declare Niamh the winner of the final round. As Nathan placed the winner's sash around her she embraced him wildly. Then she turned to the audience, bowed and enjoyed the enthusiastic applause before setting off for the catering tent with her friends, accompanied by cheers.

MUSIC CONTEST

"Dear friends," Nathan began. "I have sad news and I have good news. There will be no individual piping contest today. All of the potential participants have jointly declared that they will forgo it. A battle of the bands will take place instead. Each band has a base drummer, a snare drummer and three pipers. Both groups of musicians will alternate, playing three tunes, while they march. The scores are determined by audience votes. A small keg of moorland mead[15] awaits the winners." Nathan cleared his throat and continued, "And now I ask the audience to move to the loch shore to ensure that the formations have sufficient space for their performances."

Within minutes, onlookers and players had taken up their positions. Caitlin and Holly had Daniel between them, Ross stood behind with them with the snare drum, followed by Callum, who had strapped on the enormous bass drum. The guests stuck to the same pattern. Cat Bluebell and Lucy flanked Jack Cross, followed by John McMullen in the second row and Dongdong in the third. Upon a signal from Nathan, the marching band from the Grampian Mountains began to play.

Dongdong twirled the drumsticks above his head and John beat out a drum roll. Cat, Lucy and Jack sounded their drones[16] and began the melody on the next beat. They first marked time

---

[15] Moorland mead = A mead made by the sheep from wild honey.
[16] Drones = Reeds in bagpipes that produce a constant tone.

in place. When the refrain began, they started to move at a steady pace. Only Dongdong was in a hurry. He stomped in time with his beat, while the others had chosen to march at half tempo. Dongdong had quickly closed the distance from the rear row and crowded John McMullen from behind. Before John could protest, Dongdong had already rolled past the pipers. With closed eyes and a rapid step, Dongdong strode toward the audience. John had succeeded in escaping to the side. Together with Cat, Lucy and Jack, he followed the extraordinary spectacle.

In view of the threat, the audience parted. Dongdong marched swiftly into the loch. Moisture and cold achieved what the sheep had failed to do. Dongdong halted. He opened his eyes in amazement and stared at the surrounding water for several seconds. Then he turned around and ran, drumming, back to his band. However, they had also lost the musical competition and the match point was awarded to the home band without any real struggle.

Now it was the turn of the 'First Heather Company', as the MacAngus clan band named itself. Callum twirled his drumsticks and Ross set the beat while the three pipers topped up the air in the bags of their pipes. A command in a low voice set the band in motion. After a few measured steps, the music started. They marched to within a short distance of the audience and marked time until the pipers turned and passed around Ross and Callum.

Then the drummers turned and they all marched together to the starting point. Once there, they smoothly repeated the maneuver. While the First Heather Company received their well-deserved applause, their competitors engaged in heated discussions.

With a bright red face, an agitated John McMullen turned to Nathan. "For reasons that cannot be mentioned in public, I withdraw our participation in the pipes and drums competition. Your squad won. Congratulations."

John had hardly spoken these words before turning to his musicians and waving them from the venue. Nathan and the FHC members looked on with as much surprise as the audience. The clan chief announced the winner and requested another tune. The First Heather Company did not need to be asked twice. They played and drummed for all they were worth. As they marched off towards the catering tent, the audience followed with enthusiasm.

PRESS-O-WAR

By early afternoon it was finally time. Head butting, the most prestigious discipline in the Sheep Games, was announced. All the rams were at the start. Elimination took place sheep to sheep. Everyone drew a number. In the first round, odd numbers battled with even numbers in numerical order.

Conner had ticket number 3. Ryan had number 5. Jamie and Carl were not allowed to compete; physically, they were no match for the others.

The first match put Ross MacAngus against Jack Cross. Both rams were in their prime and in excellent physical condition. They took up positions on either side of a line drawn in the sand. At Nathan's signal they lowered their heads. A loud "Go!" indicated the beginning of the battle.

Ross and Jack crashed foreheads and held this position. They pushed with equal force and for several minutes neither had a clear advantage. But then Jack pushed forward bit by bit until he stepped over the line with his foreleg. Ross relented and Jack pushed him backwards. So Jack Cross entered the next round.

Conner and Dongdong were next to meet. Nathan stepped over to the contestants.

"Are you ready?" he asked.

Conner nodded resolutely. Dongdong grinned. "Absholootly! Ah'm fitt as a fiiddle!"

Nathan and Conner recoiled.

"Wow, that's some whisky breath," Conner said almost reverently and took a step backward.

"You can not compete in this condition. I will not allow it. John, can you confirm my decision?" Nathan asked. John McMullen had no objections, so Conner won a technical victory.

While Carl sought to convince Dongdong to take a nap, Ben and Hamish had already taken up positions opposite each other at the venue.

"Do you really want to go up against me? You'd best go back to your mum and wait one more year," Hamish taunted. Ben said nothing and lowered his head to show he was ready to begin. Nathan saw this and gave the order to start. They both put all their strength into the head butt. There was a loud crack followed by a short scream. At the last moment, before the collision, Hamish had turned his head slightly and his left horn crashed right into Ben's cheekbone. Within seconds, Ben's right eye was swollen shut and hurt terribly. But his anger outdid the pain. In a foaming rage, Ben braced himself against his devious opponent. He pushed and shoved as hard as he could, but Hamish stood as firm as a rock. On the contrary, instead of finally yielding, Hamish pressed forward inch by inch until Ben could no longer resist the pressure. Hamish had won. While Megan and Conner took care of Ben, Hamish strutted over to his fans.

The final match in the first round put Daniel MacAngus up against William Muir. The

Grampian athlete won a fair, though unexciting, contest.

Conner and Jack met head-to-head after a short pause for refreshment. Conner was still fresh and highly motivated, because there had only been victors from the Grampian flock so far. He did not count his own unopposed advance.

Each ram fixed his gaze on the other. Jack was first to lower his head. As Conner dropped his head Nathan gave the order to begin. Swift as an arrow, Conner butted. Jack appeared to be surprised as much by the speed of the charge as by its intensity. Conner exploited his advantage and continued to push with all his strength. His hind legs dug into the soil and he gained a neck's length. He still sensed Jack Cross's surprise, so Conner gathered all his strength and achieved the unexpected. He pushed Jack backwards and crossed the line. He had won! The cheers from his flock were deafening. Visibly fatigued, but proud, he went to his audience.

Nathan called up the next contestants. Hamish and William, both from the Grampian flock, approached each other. While William slowly lowered his head, Hamish again looked around with a grin. At the first indication that he too was ready for battle, Nathan called "Go!" and William butted. Before Hamish could resist, William had already pushed him back. Seconds later, Hamish sat on the ground and William stood over him. It almost looked as if he wanted to give Hamish a good hiding, but then, without a word, he went over to the chief of his clan. His chief nodded with a satisfied expression.

Nathan also nodded approval and then called upon the finalists to take up positions. "Competing for Clan MacAngus; Conner MacSheep. And for Clan McMullen; Willam Muir. We look forward to a fair contest. May the best sheep win."

After this verbose announcement, the opponents took up their starting positions. They lowered their heads at the same time and leaped forward on the order to start. Their horns crashed into each other. They pushed and shoved with all their might. Conner was able to resist the more experienced William for a short time, but then had to yield, step by step. William's triumph was unstoppable. When both of them turned to their audience, they were met with loud cheers.

"I would never have thought that you could resist me for so long," William said approvingly and gave Conner a friendly slap on the shoulder. "My respects!"

Conner was highly delighted by this recognition, but even more excited by the reception his flock had prepared for him. "Conner is the greatest" mixed with "Go Conner" rang in his ears. Then they all went to the refreshments tent to revive themselves before the hill race.

Hill Race

Anyone with four legs could participate in the Hill Race. The course, a good mile in length, had to be run in the shortest possible time. Namely, from Fairy Glen to the top of the nearest hill and, of course, back again. Any hindrances along the course had to somehow be leaped over, circumvented or waded through. To improve the odds, there were winners in three age groups; lambs, ewes and rams up to two years of age, and everyone else.

Since a small group of sheep had become lost in the previous year, the course had now been marked with special care. Even though no one seriously believed that the ewes had become lost because of insufficient trail signage. Presumably, they were too preoccupied with themselves to pay attention to the route.

A throng of excited participants waited at the start and finish line for the starter's signal. Jamie and Carl stood in the front row. They sped off at the first drumbeat. The others followed, almost as a single body. But this changed with the fording of the Black Water. The brave ones simply kept running, while those who did not care for water took a more sedate approach. Ellie and Olivia also halted at the stream. After a brief dispute, Ellie stomped onward into the cold waters.

"Well, come on!" she called to her hesitant sister. "The worst that can happen is your belly will get a little wet. There is no possibility of drowning."

"You know how much I have loathed water since I almost drowned that time," Olivia replied. "Not everyone is as crazy as you are about getting wet."

"You also don't need to wash, but I would like to carry on. So, are you coming?" Ellie pressed, with audible displeasure in her voice. Olivia listened more closely. This tone was not at all like Ellie, who was meekness personified.

"I do not believe I can do it," Olivia complained, dramatizing. And to tempt Ellie a little more, she continued, "Let us just turn back and have a bite to eat. My stomach is already queasy," she slyly enticed.

Ellie eyed her sister intently for a short time and then turned away. "Then you shall just have to turn around," she called tersely and set off.

Olivia did not understand. What had happened to Ellie? The one who was always there if Olivia needed her, or pretended to, was now following her own wishes? Could this have anything to do with Jack Cross? Olivia had certainly noticed the glances that they exchanged. Lost in thought, Olivia continued on her way. Her musings had distracted her so much from her fear of water that she was not even aware of how she reached the other bank. Ellie was already out of sight, so Olivia went on, alone and silent, behind the runners. It was only when Dongdong, panting loudly, overtook her that she fell into a gentle trot and concentrated on the hill race.

Nathan and John McMullen observed the contestants from the tower in the castle ruins. After their initial sprint, Jamie and Carl had slowed and then been absorbed by the main body of runners. Heroes of previous competitions and new contestants jostled in this group. Everything from friendly comments to calls of encouragement for the faltering could be heard. Overall, it was more of an enjoyable group activity than a competition, but everyone was pleased. When Conner and his friends reached the highest point on the racecourse they jumped in the air for joy and, hooting, started back down the path. They bounded over bushes and small cliffs and some of them felt as if they could fly. Ellie was not quite such a fleet-footed runner, but she pressed on. Side-by-side with Jack Cross, she took the turn and skipped downhill like a baby lamb, despite small aches. Ellie beamed with happiness. Nor did Jack Cross look precisely sad.

The last section of the course was also flat and called for a sprint. Conner, Ben, Daniel and Callum attempted to outdo each other. Completely out of breath, Conner was first over the finish line. The others followed close on his heels. Cheering loudly, the young rams leaped around and then went off to the refreshment tent together. Jamie was next to finish. Despite tired legs he bounced among the audience like a rubber ball. Megan reeled him in and, as a paramedic, prescribed an urgent, large gulp of water. As a proud mother, she treated him to a mug of blueberry juice as a reward.

Little by little returning runners first filled the finish area and then the refreshment tent. When the last runner, a red-faced Dongdong, arrived after a long gap, Nathan MacAngus and John McMullen also went into the tent for refreshment.

PATTERN NIBBLING

The last competition of the day took place on the lush lawn behind the castle ruins. Nathan assigned each participant—only ewes had registered—to a four sheep-length by four sheep-length square. Here, they would graze and create a free-form pattern in the grass. Lucy and Cat Bluebell kicked off for the Grampians; Ellie and Holly for Clan MacAngus.

Nathan greeted the large number of exuberant onlookers and gave the order to start. In a flash, four heads dropped and the ewes began with the coarse clipping. Lucy and Holly were beginners in this contest and restricted themselves to a simple One-Line-Knot pattern[17], while Cat Bluebell attempted a D-Ring pattern[18].

At the outset, Ellie's work conveyed nothing to the audience, but when she began the detailed work a murmur ran through the crowd. Ellie gnawed and nibbled a modified panel knot[19]. In addition to the doubled knots, two hearts were intertwined on the left and right sides of the top. Lucy and Holly were the first to end their work, followed by Cat. When the audience broke out in rhythmic clapping during Ellie's final embellishing munches, the winner was already clear. While Nathan confirmed Ellie as the winner, she and Jack gazed deeply into each other's eyes. Ellie's opponents congratulated her with a wink. Then everyone rushed to the tent in order to bring this eventful day to its grand finale.

THE CELEBRATION

After everyone had eaten and drunk, the dance band assembled. Dongdong was sober

---

[17] One-Line-Knot-Pattern = Classic Celtic knot pattern
[18] D-Ring-Pattern = Classic Celtic knot pattern based on a 'D'
[19] Panel knot = Complex repeating Celtic knot pattern

again after the hill race and played the bass drum. Ross took over the snare drum and Cat Bluebell, Holly and Daniel played the bagpipes. By the second tune, the dance floor was crowded. Conner, Ben, Abbie and Kathie danced exuberantly in a circle. Caitlin and Lucy sought to outdo Niamh and Lauren in step dancing. Olivia was invited by John McMullen and Sarah danced by herself. Ellie and Jack only had eyes for each other. From time to time the dancers changed partners or reformed for a round dance. The mood was magnificent.

Under the influence of adrenaline and Grandsheep's Best whisky, Ellie grabbed a snare drum and completely amazed the dancers. On top of this, Olivia performed a fiery Sword Dance and created just as much astonishment.

Caitlin clapped enthusiastically. "When you see Olivia like this, it's easy to imagine that she was really sought after at one time," she said to Megan. "Perhaps she would have been quite different if things had gone well with Conner back then."

"Conner?" Megan asked inquisitively. "Tell me, you secretive thing," she insisted.

"Ach, I don't know all the details. But Conner, that is, my Conner MacSheep, not my son, had a love affair with Olivia before my time. She was very much in love, but Conner was always simply a terrific lover; not a faithful soul." Caitlin sighed in fond reminiscence.

"Well, when Olivia became jealous – with good reason, by the way – and displayed it very clearly, Conner jilted her and I became his wife." Then she laughed mischievously. "But, as you know, that was also only for a short time. Still, better short and sweet than not at all."

At a late hour, Cat Bluebell began to sing the old ballad of Kieran and Heather. Everyone listened raptly to this story of love and revenge, longing and fulfillment, clan feuds and reconciliation in the Scottish Highlands. But that is a story unto itself.

The First Full Moon

The sensational days of the games and the celebration were over and calm had returned to the pasture. Conner and Abbie walked together through Fairy Glen, always followed by Jamie. Since Conner's magnificent victory, he apparently only had one thing in mind: to be Conner's most devoted fan.

Nevertheless, if the couple succeeded in shaking him off, they disappeared into the Little Glen, the name they had given to their secret valley. Today, for example. In high spirits, Abbie skipped over the low wall of the abandoned cottage and began her favorite game.

"Turn around so I can hide," she called to Conner. "And then you must look for me!"

Conner obediently turned his back to her.

"O.K. Now you can start."

Abbie jumped behind a boulder where several small birches grew. It gave her a hiding place, but was still comfortable. With a short bleat she indicated that she was now ready to be found.

Conner looked behind the wall and then ducked away. Stooping, he crept from behind toward the boulder where Abbie crouched in suspense. With one bound, Conner was beside her and playfully pinched her ear.

"Got you," he announced triumphantly.

"You peeked," Abbie protested loudly and searched for Conner's most ticklish spot. Conner defended himself and switched over to further tickling and nibbling onslaughts. They tumbled and rolled more and more wildly across the meadow. Suddenly their lips touched and, responding to the world's oldest reflex, kissed. For several seconds, their world stopped turning.

Then they flew apart as if burned. Embarrassed, they turned away from each other. Abbie was first to regain composure.

"Shall we play something else?" she asked as if nothing had happened and turned to face him.

"No", Conner mumbled, but looked in her direction again.

"We could play tag or race each other."

"No, I'm no longer interested," Conner said and kicked a few pebbles.

"Why not? I would like to. Just do it for my sake and you'll find out that you like it, too."

"I already said that I don't want to, so kindly

leave me in peace," Conner replied brusquely and ran a few steps away from her. "I'm going home. You can come with me or stay here, whichever you want," Conner said and set off without waiting for her reply.

Abbie was bewildered. She had never seen Conner like this before. At first, everything had been fun and all right, then they had even kissed and now he was suddenly unpredictable. Shaken, she ran after him.

Arriving at the pasture, they went their separate ways. In search of comfort, Abbie ran to her mother. Conner stumped over to the young rams from the flock and gladly became involved in a discussion about the games. He laughed and talked a little too loudly, but that did not bother the others.

For the first time, a day ended uncomfortably for Conner and Abbie.

As night drew in, each sheep sought out a cozy spot to bed down. Some liked to sleep close together, others preferred their own spot. As always, Conner lay close to his family. He was already nodding off when the moon rose slowly in the sky. Silvery light struck his eyes and he was suddenly wide-awake. He felt a powerful restlessness within and an indescribable desire for something that he could not name. He got up with shaking legs and quietly crept up the hill above the resting sheep.

Reaching the top, he looked up at the sky

and froze. The moon's enormous silvery disc sent its hypnotic beams directly into Conner's head. Without thinking, he obeyed an irresistible inner urge and bleated as loud and long as he could. At the same time, his ears stood up like a hare's and gleamed, pale pink in the moonlight. Thousands of tiny, voracious devils that he could not pacify erupted in his belly. What was happening to him?

All night long, he walked the hills around Fairy Glen. He attempted to satisfy his longing with juicy grass, but tonight it tasted as stale as ancient hay. He tried herbs and flower buds. Even heather did not go unscathed. The only thing he felt was mild nausea, followed by an even greater urge. The marvelous cool water of the Black Water River did not help him.

Worst of all, these bleating fits overtook him again and again. Each gruesome sound seemed to make its way through his throat unaided. His chin stretched upwards and from his wide-open mouth came sounds that gave every Highlander goose bumps.

When dawn finally broke, he felt absolutely miserable and crept back to his sleeping spot. Trembling and exhausted from the sleepless night, he fell into a dreamless sleep.

New Knowledge

After Conner was completely rested, the days and nights went by with their usual routine. The young rams teased the young ewes and the older ones held their little chats.

Olivia made an issue of only one topic, the horrendous night of the full moon. At every opportunity she speculated, whether appropriate or not, about "that howling", as she called it. At this very moment, she was talking again to a group of young ewes.

"I shall never forget that time, when stones rained from the heavens and the four-horned one called out. For a moment the blood froze in my veins and I was sure that our end had come." Olivia enjoyed the terror in the eyes of the younger sheep.

"Of course. And once the thunderstorm and hail was over, we danced a country waltz with the four-horned one," Ellie said, interrupting the horror session.

Olivia was indignant. "You'll see. One of these days it will be upon us and there will be no mercy!" she prophesied and glared aggressively at the group.

But Ellie had broken the spell. The listeners moved off, laughing, and Olivia's threats deflated in the afternoon sun.

As before, Conner and Abbie played and frolicked and visited Little Glen from time to time. Only sometimes, for a few seconds, a strange shyness intruded on their togetherness.

Caitlin watched the starry sky every evening and tracked the moon's phases. One day, shortly before sunset, she called Conner to her side.

"This evening, we are going to pay another visit to Dun Eagle. Nathan is coming with us." and added, as if she had anticipated Conner's thoughts, "Right now."

Caitlin's tone tolerated no objection, and they set off. The elderly Nathan made only slow progress. So darkness was falling as they reached the castle ruins.

Cool and majestic, the silvery disc of the moon rose above the ruined tower. Suddenly, Conner's innards tightened convulsively. He again felt the moon's light in his head. His ears pricked up and gleamed, pale pink. He stopped, stiff legged, raised his chin and threw out a gruesome, prolonged bleat.

Caitlin and Nathan observed Conner for a short time. Then Caitlin ran to him and embraced him gently, but firmly.

"My little darling," she whispered. "That is your father's legacy and the curse of the MacSheeps. Come with me to Nathan, because you need to know what is happening to you."

Together, they entered the shadows of the ruins, where Nathan awaited them.

"Sit down and listen to me," Nathan began. Conner felt the restlessness within himself and could hardly imagine sitting here quietly. But his curiosity was aroused, so he suppressed his urge to move.

"Many years ago, when this ruin was still an occupied castle, a small flock of Highland sheep like us lived by this loch. Their clan chief was an ancestor of mine. There was also a MacSheep called Aidan in this flock.

The MacSheeps had always lived with other clans, because they were not numerous enough to defend themselves without allies. But they were always welcome in our clan. Aidan was an adventurer with an eye for the ladies and always ready for a prank. Nevertheless, one day he disappeared without a word. When he turned up again, after a long time, he was unrecognizable. He was completely emaciated. His fleece was filthy and matted. But looking into his eyes was the worst. Before, they had really shone, but now they were dull. In fact, almost lifeless."

Nathan took a small flask from his sporran[20], drank a sip and passed it to Conner.

"That's uisge-beatha[21]," he explained. "A small sip is medicinal, but beware of too much, because that will be your ruin."

Conner looked questioningly at Caitlin. She nodded. He took a small sip and passed the flask to Caitlin. Hell! This water of life burned fiercely in his mouth. He swallowed it quickly. From the burning, he could feel exactly where it was. Then the traces of fire transformed into a large warm belly and his legs grew heavy.

Nathan continued. "When Aidan got the moon sickness, as it was called, no one knew where it came from or how to cure it. Aidan suffered terribly until he learned what satisfied his craving. But when he made that discovery, he found it unbearable. He left the flock that very night and only returned years later. In the meantime, he had suppressed his longing with uisge beatha, but had become accustomed to his "rescuer" over time. He drank more and more and not only on full moon nights. He was driven away from the settlements and no flock was willing to take him in. Alone, he wandered in the trackless areas. The grass grew sparsely there and he became weaker and weaker. With his

---

[20] Sporran (Gaelic) = Traditional fur or leather pouch worn at the waist with Highland dress, since kilts have no pockets.
[21] Uisge-beatha (Gaelic) = Water of Life, an old term for whisky.

last strength, he returned home."

Nathan sighed heavily. "He died not long after that and took his secret with him to his grave."

Conner sat as if turned to stone. What would become of him? Could he fight the moon sickness? Or must he also flee from his family and live alone in the mountains like Aidan? What would Abbie think of him? Oh, Abbie! Conner felt a warmth in his belly. If only she were here!

"Don't worry, Conner! Nathan and I shall take good care of you, " Caitlin said.

"But we know absolutely nothing about this moon sickness," Conner objected. "Sometimes Olivia makes such strange insinuations..."

"You certainly should never take Olivia seriously. First, she exaggerates outrageously and second, she believes that there is some kind of unsettled score between us," Caitlin sputtered.

"Well, the sickness undoubtedly affects others just as it touches you," Nathan said soberly, joining in again. "When the full moon rises you start to bleat for all you are worth. And you know better than I what else happens to you."

Nathan and Caitlin looked at him questioningly.

"I feel an uncanny longing inside. My stomach gets tight. I must swallow constantly. Suddenly, grass and herbs no longer taste good and even water from the Black Water is no help. I never felt anything like this before," Conner recounted and blushed immediately, because he lied. He had felt almost exactly the same when he kissed Abbie. But he could not and would not say that now. That was his secret.

"It was like that with your father," Caitlin said quietly. "Sadly, he only confided in me a little. But he was quite certain that he could not satisfy his longing here in the Highlands. That is why he disappeared shortly before you were born."

"But what are Olivia's insinuations about," Conner wanted to know.

Caitlin evaded his question. "That is not so important, simply gossip and exaggeration."

"Despite that, I want to know, "Conner insisted.

Nathan tried to intervene and help, but Caitlin waved him off. "He has a right to find out, even if they are only rumors and the worst kind of gossip," she conceded. "For a time, it was claimed that your father disappeared because he allegedly attacked other sheep—lambs—on full moon nights," Caitlin said with a tremulous voice, "and drank their blood. Someone claimed that lambs had been found with torn throats. At the full moon, naturally. And they boldly claimed that Conner was responsible." She shook with anger. "Just because he was not with the flock at the full moon and howled at it as you do. As if there were no wolves or stray dogs that could have done it." She took a deep breath to calm herself, without success. "They wanted to harm him and make him look bad out of pure envy and jealousy," she grumbled, until Nathan interrupted her.

"Hold on, Caitlin, you are only making the lad more confused," Nathan soothed. "It is true that there were several dead lambs at the time, but how they died remained unknown. And, like every story, many made up something to add to it. You were Conner's wife, but he did not even tell you what he got up to on full moon nights. We should look after his son instead of continuing to speculate about what might have been."

"You are right, Nathan," Caitlin said. She then turned to Conner with a firm voice. "Promise us that you not act rashly under any circumstances," Caitlin demanded. "Most of all, do not simply run away! We shall find a way to deal with this legacy."

Conner promised.

Back To Bettyhill

It grew colder in the days and weeks that followed. The morning mist turned directly into evening fog, interrupted only by midday drizzle. The flock sought shelter in the old Dun Eagle ruin. They stood tightly packed. For the first few days they continued to talk about the sheep games and the fantastic closing celebration. But ultimately, the most impressive buck vaulting and most beautiful patterns had been described and admired sufficiently from every viewpoint. The overall mood sank. The days dragged by, slowly and monotonously, until loud whistling, calls and barking sounded one morning.

"Adam is here. We are going home." The sheep rejoiced and rushed into the open.

"Ah, there you are, my beauties," Adam said with relief. "I was afraid that I would have to look for you all over the glen."

A chorus of bleating answered him. Sparky, the elderly Border collie, had a chat with Nathan and Ellie.

"Adam has become a modern shepherd. He

now has a scooter."

"What does he do with it?" Ellie asked.

"You'll soon see. In any case, it means that he does not need a second sheep dog," Sparky explained. "He herds the flock almost singlehanded with Clunker, as he calls the scooter."

"How will he..." Ellie began, when a noisy roar interrupted her. The terrified animals ran in the opposite direction. Adam followed the flock on Clunker. Sparky flushed out the stragglers and herded them into the large throng.

The flock spent the entire day in motion. Towards evening, they finally reached the home pasture with its spacious byre at the edge of Bettyhill. Now, the sheep only differed in their level of fatigue. And after a few mouthfuls of grass they all sought a place to sleep.

The next morning began with a surprise. Adam had brought two more men. Large plastic sacks were stacked alongside the byre and a generator hummed evenly.

One animal after another was led to the humming side of the byre, set on their bottom and ... sheared. By evening, every sheep had "lost weight" and was freezing. But Adam was a good shepherd. He had spread straw in the byre and provided a bale of the finest hay for dinner. The animals accepted the offer gratefully.

Little happened in the days that followed. A large low-pressure system brought the first steady rain of fall to Scotland, accompanied by further cooling. The sheep ate and slept all day long.

"How are they still able to sleep at night?" Conner asked in a murmur.

"I have no idea," Abbie answered. "But I'm not tired at all. I believe that I have slept enough for the next 100 years."

"Then you feel like I do. Anyway, I'm not going into the byre this evening to sleep. I'm going to do something. Are you coming with me?"

Abbie was about to raise an undoubtedly very sensible protest when she recalled the snoring and corrosive boredom of the previous night. She resolutely swallowed her doubts.

"I'll come with you," she said and confirmed her decision with a vigorous nod.

"Then lay down a little to the side to sleep, so we can slip out, unnoticed. I'll give you a sign when it is time."

Abbie was so excited that she could only nod. Conner winked at her and strolled over to Ben, who he nudged amiably. Abbie attempted to conceal her restlessness with merry chatter.

As the sun set, the sheep trotted into the byre and lay down. After a short time, the space was filled with the sound of snuffling and snoring. Conner raised his head and nodded to Abbie. She returned his nod. They crept out together.

Oh, this was wonderful! The sky was overcast but the air was cold and clear. In silence, they walked alongside each other to the road. Then the spell broke. They laughed away their tension and frisked around boisterously.

"Look, there are lights down there," Conner cried and ran faster. Halfway down the hill, he was seized by a spasm and stopped suddenly. His chin flew upwards and a horrific bleating tore the night silence. By the moon's light, Abbie saw Conner as a dark shadow. His ears pointed directly upwards. His head stretched toward the full moon and a continuous sound, painful to the ear, flowed from his mouth.

For a moment, Abbie paused, transfixed by this extraordinary sight. Then she shook herself and ran to him.

"Conner, hey, Conner," she called insistently. "Look at me. Don't look at the moon."

Conner heard the concern in Abbie's words. With enormous willpower, he severed the connection to the moon's hypnotic disc. "Abbie, I... I didn't know," he stammered. "Did I frighten you?"

"You can say that again," Abbie replied. "What's wrong with you?"

"Mum and Nathan call it the moon sickness. But I don't believe that they know very much about it. And I also haven't had it for long. It seems to have something to do with our clan, the MacSheeps. It only happens when the moon is full and by the next day it is gone. I didn't know that it would be today, otherwise I wouldn't have taken you with me."

"What nonsense," Abbie shouted angrily. "Am I nothing more than a pretty face to you? You don't trust me?"

"Oh, no, Abbie! You know that you are my best friend. You are definitely much more than just a pretty face."

Conner closed his eyes and pressed close to Abbie. He raised his head and ... kissed her. Hot and cold shivers passed through him. His restlessness turned to tingling anticipation. When he opened his eyes again, the moon had disappeared behind a cloud. Abbie stood in front of him with a flushed face. Her eyes sparkled like stars in the sky.

"I like that," she said in a low voice. "But I think we should keep going now, before a human sees us."

Conner also had a lump in his throat and merely nodded. Lost in thought, they strolled toward the lights. As they came closer, they realized that only the streetlights were lit. The houses were dark. Only sparse light passed through gaps in the shutters. However, exterior lighting burned at one house. Conner went purposefully toward it. Abbie followed close behind. On the front of the house, illuminated by the lamp, hung an enamel sign with a large letter **i,** promising information for tourists. Alongside it, displayed in a showcase, was a paper with a few colors and many lines. The two adventurers suddenly heard voices from the interior of the house. A man and a woman were talking. Frightened, Conner and Abbie ducked against the wall under the window. While Conner was still considering how they could get out of this situation without being seen, an incredibly delicious aroma wafted into his nose.

Never in his life had he smelled anything so fine, caressing the stomach and soul at the same time. In ecstasy, he closed his eyes and drew in as much as he could. The window under which they cowered suddenly opened. Someone closed the shutters and then closed the window again. A door clicked and the man and woman departed.

Abbie exhaled deeply. "Wow, that was close!" she whispered and looked expectantly at Conner. But he had only one goal. He simply had to find out what exuded this extraordinary aroma. Cautiously he crept along the wall and looked around the corner. There was no one in sight. He signaled Abbie to follow him and crept over to the door—closed! Disappointed, he turned to Abbie, but she was no longer visible. Conner peered helplessly into the darkness.

Then the door opened, as if by an unseen hand. "Won't you come in?" Abbie asked innocently.

More than astonished, Conner stepped inside. "How did you do that?" he asked.

"Quite easy. There is a window next to the large sign and it was open." She beamed at him. "I also found out where the fine aroma comes from. It's from the kitchen. I'll show you."

She confidently pulled Conner into a room. Instantly a veritable cloud of aroma surrounded them. As if drawn by a magnet, Conner headed for the source of bliss. A still-warm chocolate cake stood in moonlight on the kitchen table. With a hoarse groan, he fell upon the confection and licked up the warm chocolate coating. Then he licked his mouth appreciatively, closed his eyes and bit off a sizable portion. He chewed and smacked his lips, wolfed down and swallowed until only a few crumbs remained on the plate. An indescribably pleasant sensation ran through him. Satisfied, he opened his eyes and saw a very disconcerted Abbie before him.

"That was quick," was all Abbie could think of. "But thank you. I really didn't want any."

"Och, Abbie. You can't imagine how delicious that was. I never imagined there could be anything so wonderful," Conner said with a broad grin. "Let's see if there are any more delicacies like this."

Abbie was understanding and joined him in

the search. They found lots of dishes and pots and a great white chest that hummed, but could not be opened. Full of hope, they turned to the other rooms. Several small tables and chairs stood in one of them and a stairway led from its center to the upper floor. Numerous pictures hung on the walls and brightly colored wool socks, gloves and scarves lay on shelves. A small white ticket carrying symbols that Abbie and Conner could not decipher was stuck to every item.

As reserved as Abbie had been during the cake eating, now she really opened up. She took the brightest scarf and wound it around her neck. Then she placed socks and gloves on her hooves and strutted through the house. She found a mirror where she could admire her new look. Many colors suited her.

Meanwhile, Conner had found small bags and strived to get at their contents. When he finally succeeded numerous red and white balls rolled out and several went down the stairs. Curious, Conner sampled several of them at once. They tasted uncommonly fresh and chilled his mouth like cold river water, but at their centers chocolate soothed the taste buds.

The two investigators were so absorbed by their discoveries that they only noticed the loud rumbling in front of the house when light suddenly came through the window.

The 'Scotsman'[22] van stopped on its morning round to deliver its cargo. Conner and Abbie leaped from the window in sheer panic. They crossed the road and ran across the meadows toward the byre as quickly as they could. Shortly before reaching it they stopped, panting. Only then did Abbie notice that she had lost her gloves and one of the socks. Only the scarf remained in place, thanks to the ample knot. Conner looked at her with a broad grin.

"You never told me that you were feeling cold," he teased. Abbie looked at him. Conner tapped her neck.

She let out an "Oh. I didn't think any more about it." Then she looked down at herself. "I must have lost the other things while running," she conjectured.

"I don't think that's so bad, but you should wear this scarf more often. It really suits you."

Abbie felt herself blush. Just then, of all times, the moon came out from behind a cloud. Conner raised his gaze to the sky and felt a slight tingling in his belly. But he had no urge to bleat and his head was clear. Satisfied with his condition and the outcome of their adventure, he and Abbie slipped into the byre.

---

[22] The Scotsman = Scottish daily newspaper

Moonlight And November Blues

The days grew shorter and colder. Abbie regretted that she could not wear her pretty colored scarf. But then she would have to explain where it came from and that, in turn, was impossible without lying. Lying to someone, especially her parents, was out of the question for Abbie. So freezing was the only choice left to her. In the rare moments when she felt unobserved, she took her plunder from its hiding place and gazed at it wistfully.

One day Janet returned from a walk and received a great deal of attention because of her souvenir. An opportunity to be the center of attention had not arisen for a very long time. She therefore gladly took on the task of telling everyone the story of the dangerous sock rescue. The whole affair became more dramatic with every repetition. Finally she told her story to Ellie and Olivia.

"So," she began, "I had already covered a strenuous stretch on my walk when I reached a fence. There were several rows of wire connected to a battery. The fence hummed rather noisily.

Behind it stood or lay about twenty of those shaggy Highland cattle. With those long pointed horns, they looked very dangerous."

Janet made a brief pause and enjoyed her listeners' attentiveness. "Then I noticed this colorful stocking in the middle of the pasture. I thought for a moment. Then I crouched so low that I could slip under the lowest wire and into the meadow. I crept unobtrusively past the cattle, snatched up the stocking and slipped back under the wire as quickly as I could. It's a pity that I went to all that trouble for only one sock. If there had been two, I could wear them now and again."

"You can always warm one foot at a time," the practically-oriented Ellie suggested.

"Of course, you could also insert two feet and hop around like a kangaroo," Olivia said tartly and turned away, shaking her head.

Poor Janet was so bewildered that she was unable to respond. Ellie comforted her with a tap on the shoulder and went off 'for a bite' as she murmured to Janet.

Conner and Abbie doubled over with laughter at the notion of Janet creeping and slithering. Given her girth, it certainly was an outstanding performance. Nevertheless, Janet's stocking story remained the day's only diversion. As the last daylight disappeared, even the most bored sheep went into the byre. It did not take long until the sounds of sleep emanated from every corner.

As a precaution, Conner waited a little longer and then crept out. He took a deep breath. Tonight, he wanted to venture further from his home. He preferred to tell Abbie nothing, since she would surely have been against it.

So now he traveled the road to Ullapool alone. He knew nothing about the place, but he had also known nothing about Bettyhill, so he would try his luck. Now and then he met a car but there was no need to hide. The humans were accustomed to ewes and rams wandering freely and did not worry about it.

Reaching Ullapool, he kept to the darkest streets and suddenly stood at the harbor. Tightly packed fishing boats were moored at the quay. They swayed with the waves and the wind blew a peculiar tune in their rigging. Conner looked around in fascination. On the far side, the houses were lined up like pearls on a string. The ground-floor shop windows were dark. Light shone from only a few windows on the upper floors.

Conner crossed the street as quietly as he could and began window-shopping. He gazed in wonder at fish traps and angling equipment, books and toys. One shop offered immense quantities of kilts and plaids, another had very few items, but they glittered and gleamed. They were reminiscent of Sparky's collar, but it was unlikely that these were intended for dogs. They were too small.

When he reached the last of the houses his whole belly suddenly cramped and he had to sit for a moment. He not only felt hungry, he felt as if he were starving. At the same time, a wild craving arose in his belly. He leaned backwards to stand up and fell heavily into a hallway. Dazed, he sat up and tried to orient himself. Various doors went off to the left and right. He took a chance and tried the nearest one. It would not open. Neither did the next door or the one after that, but then came a swinging door.

Conner literally flew into the room. Fortunately he was able to stop in front of the table, where bowls and plates stood. He stood like a statue and held his breath. When he was sure that no one had heard him, his tension diminished. He went around the table, examining the contents of the bowls. He could not identify it, but he did not feel any attraction.

Disappointed, he was about to leave when he heard a familiar hum. He turned around and stood in front of an enormous white chest like the one in Bettyhill. This one also did not appear to have a handle, but after searching Conner found a crack where he could insert his front hoof. He pulled with all his might. The refrigerator door opened with a crack and released indescribably wonderful aromas.

A true paradise lay before him in the

glistening light. He removed a bowl as carefully as he could. The smell reminded him of the chocolate cake, but the contents were creamy and cold. Oh, how delectable! Again and again he dipped his tongue into the chocolate pudding until his worst cravings were satisfied.

Then he made a detailed inspection of the refrigerator. Small chocolate truffles with coconut shavings lay on one plate, chocolate-dipped mint candy on another. One bowl contained a caramel pastry and whisky honey gleamed like liquid gold in a jar.

Conner sampled, licked his lips, evaluated and then turned to the next delicacy. Several strange looking glasses with stems stood on the top shelf. They were filled with a white cream in which bright red raspberries appeared to float. Conner took out one of these glasses, sniffed at it and lapped appreciatively.

In no time at all, he had consumed five of these delicious desserts. With the sixth cranachan[23], he suddenly felt dizzy and had an urgent need for open sky and fresh air.

He stood up and went to the door. As he did so, he noticed that his legs had clearly developed a mind of their own because, although he wished to walk straight to the door, he bumped into several cabinets. Last but not least, he crashed into the table. With a loud roar, a stack of plates

---

[23] Cranachan or crowdie cream = Traditional Scottish desert with whisky.

fell to the floor and shattered.

For seconds, Conner was petrified with shock. Then a wave of adrenaline surged through him and he tumbled outside. Blindly, he ran down the street and only stopped when he felt soft ground beneath his feet. He looked around, gasping for air. There were no houses to be seen anywhere and the soft ground beneath him was sand. He had fled to the beach and, most probably, safety. Yet which direction should he take to reach home again?

All around him, darkness and silence prevailed. Only now and then did a soft splashing reach his ears. Now he also felt how his legs shook and many tiny devils danced in his stomach. He stomped laboriously through the sand and wished that he could have offered his craving at least a little resistance. Then he would not feel so queasy now.

Lost in thought, he walked for quite a while until he stumbled over something large and soft. Before he could even consider what it might be, the seal had already raised itself and struck him. Terrified, Conner stepped back, only to immediately trip over the next seal.

Fortunately, the moon broke through the clouds at that moment and lit up the beach. Conner raised his chin toward the moon and a drawn out bleat that could be heard for miles surged from his throat. The seal herd sought salvation by fleeing to the sea. Once again,

Conner was alone on the beach.

He used this opportunity to orient himself and set off in a new direction. He stomped up the sandy hill and reached the road. Now in good spirits, he followed it and reached his home byre.

When he had made himself comfortable in his sleeping spot he smiled to himself once more. He had used the moon sickness to his advantage for the first time. On the beach, he had felt no urge to bleat, much less been compelled to do so. But when he saw the full moon he was simply able to conjure up this terrifying sound and drive the seals away.

He was very pleased with himself and the outcome of the day's adventure.

Eventful December

After Abbie had sulked – as Conner and Ben called it – for three days, she came running to them today with a mischievous grin. In spite of the continuing rain, most of the sheep remained outdoors and used the light of the short day to find the last fresh blades of grass.

As if nothing had ever happened, Abbie began, "Pay attention! I bet you that Janet will come out at any second and cause a colossal sensation."

Abbie had hardly finished when a wild bleating, interspersed with "Ah"s and "Oh"s, could be heard from the byre. Then a throng of astonished sheep, led by Janet, stepped into the open.

"A miracle has happened! Just imagine! My sock has reproduced. Now there are two. A complete pair. Early this morning, both of them suddenly lay beside my head." She triumphantly raised two colorful socks high into the air.

Most of the sheep showed no interest. Only a

few sensation seekers crowded around Janet. Abbie could hardly contain her laughter. She spluttered and giggled. Her delight was infectious. It struck Conner first. Ben was infected shortly afterwards. Curious, Kathie came running. She was infected by the good mood in a flash.

"We are so delighted by the miraculous sock reproduction," she heard between laughs. "And later on there will be another miracle," Abbie burst out, giggling.

Suddenly she became serious and said solemnly, "I would like a big warm scarf. I am sure that I'll find one on this day, blessed as it is with miracles." Abbie retained her innocent, serious expression and said to the others, "I'm now going to go and sleep a little. Perhaps the scarf will already have arrived when I wake up."

She stomped resolutely into the byre, lay down and closed her eyes. Astounded, Ben and Kathie watched her go. A premonition flashed through Conner. Was this really so wise? But it was strictly Abbie's decision, so with a shrug he turned to Ben. "Girls!" was his only comment, whereupon Kathie left the group and followed Abbie.

The flock calmed and settled down to ruminate. A little later, Abbie and Kathie came out of the byre. Each held one end of the colored scarf and called out in unison, "Look. It worked. We received a scarf as a gift."

In high spirits, they ran across the meadow with their trophy and laughed. Halfway back, Holly stepped into their path. Half annoyed, half amused, she emphatically demanded an explanation from her daughter. Abbie suddenly felt uncomfortable and turned under her mother's gaze. After some hesitation, she told about what had happened in Bettyhill. Holly then imposed a temporary halt to scarf wearing and a ban on accompanying Conner on his forays. She confiscated the scarf and went purposefully to Caitlin. Both mothers spoke to each other intently for a long time.

The anger had vanished by the next morning. The sheep stood or lay around in small groups and ate or chatted. Nothing whatsoever happened during the whole blessed day. As they all withdrew to the byre in the evening, Conner elbowed his way to Abbie.

"I'm going out tonight. Are you coming with me?" he whispered in her ear.

"I'd love to come with you, but it's better if I don't. Mum's anger has definitely blown over, but she's keeping an eye on me."

"Then just as well not to," Conner replied succinctly. "Sleep well, kid," he added in a mocking undertone before turning away.

Abbie bit her lower lip in anger. But she kept her promise and lay down next to her mother. She could not fall asleep for a long time and at one point believed she heard the byre door.

However, Conner was already on the way to Ullapool. The many shops and unknown possibilities had a magical attraction for him. The night sky was clear so he made good progress. As he turned into the harbor street, the moon rose over the range of hills behind the little town.

Conner felt the change in himself. If he did not immediately find protection from the light of the full moon, he would lose control. Then his only choice would be homeward flight and the torment of his cravings.

He saved himself at the last moment by leaping into an open hallway. Trembling from the effort, he leaned on the wall and peeked out from the front door. He discovered a large shop window across the way that only offered a small square of clear visibility because of the cold. Curious, he attempted to determine the nature of the business. He waited until he could feel his legs again and his head grew clearer. Then he ran as fast as he could to the other side.

Next to the display window, four steps led to the shop door. Conner pushed hard against it and it yielded. Quickly, he slipped into the warmth and closed the entrance door. He took a step into the room and looked around. The walls were fitted with shelves up to the ceiling. On them stood large, closely packed jars. Small objects were stored in every one. In front, a good sheep's length away, stretched a counter. It consisted mainly of glass and contained many silver trays on which diversely colored balls and cubes were stacked. An exquisite aroma from the most varied spices hung in the air. Conner inhaled with pleasure and began his inspection.

He first grabbed a jar with gold colored balls. The glass lid only sat on top, which made access easier. Conner let a couple of balls roll onto the shop counter and licked them up. They were hard and sweet and easy to bite through. From inside them, creamy chocolate flowed into his mouth. Conner moaned appreciatively and grabbed another jar. As soon as it was opened, a fruity, sharp aroma mixed with chocolate escaped. Conner reached inside and gulped down the ten chocolate-coated ginger sticks without further ado. Fabulous!

He looked around the shop again. There were a hundred delicacies to be discovered and he still had the whole night before him. He slowly went along the shelves, grabbed a jar now and then and thoroughly sampled the contents. No wish remained unfulfilled. Everything was available, from candied fruit to sherbet candy, cola lollipops, and licorice confectionery. Once he was finished with the lower two rows, he turned to the counter.

He first directed his attention to the small balls rolled in sugar, which were available in creamy white, light and dark brown. After the first truffle, there was no stopping. One after the other, he wolfed down the white, the dark and finally the light brown treats. Next he turned to the cognac filled chocolates and then the whisky truffles, smacking his lips. The strawberry cream and butter truffles also tasted excellent to him.

Becoming thirsty, he looked for something to drink. In a small closet adjoining the shop, he found an already familiar humming chest. This one was not as large as the last, but just as easy to open. Unfortunately, it did not contain any cranachan, but Conner found a dark bottle with very fizzy contents. After a few deep breaths, he belched so loud that he frightened himself. This drank only partly quenched the thirst, but it tasted delicious. So he took the bottle with him into the shop to continue his feast. After he had eaten almost the entire contents of the counter, he looked around for other flavorful challenges.

Directly opposite the entry door stood a basket with gingerbread and fruitcake. Conner freed the fruitcake from its clear plastic wrap and sniffed. Fantastic. Such a fruity, spicy aroma! He bit into it heartily, chewed, and washed it down with the fizzy drink.

When he turned once more to the shelves his legs did not obey him in the usual way. As a precaution, he got down on his knees and crawled to the Santas and candy canes on the left-hand side. He overcame the tinfoil after a brief struggle and bit heartily into the chocolate. He smacked his lips and lapped, crumbled and gurgled, until he fell asleep on a mountain of half-eaten Santas and candy canes with the champagne bottle in his arms.

Next morning, Miss Shortbread, the elderly shop owner, entered the site of destruction. Despite the noise that Conner had created shortly before his transition from drunkenness to sleep, Miss Shortbread had been unaware of the break-in. As always, she had removed her hearing aid before going to bed and was therefore virtually deaf. When her gaze fell on Conner after a brief survey of the devastation, she screamed. Conner was not a pretty sight! Not simply because he snored loudly with an open mouth. No, he was smeared with chocolate from head to foot. Conner quickly opened his eyes and instantly felt a violent headache. He groaned and attempted to sit up. The further his head traveled from the floor, the worse the pain became.

Miss Shortbread had quickly recognized that Conner did not represent any threat. On the contrary. For this poor sheep to moan this way, it must have a full-fledged hangover. She approached cautiously.

"Are you very sick? How did you get in here? And where on earth do you come from?' she asked quietly, since she still remembered quite well that someone in this condition could not tolerate loud sounds.

"Oh," she said to herself, "there I go again. Now I'm even talking to a sheep. I really am getting a little odd." She shook her head, smiling at herself. "But you know, when you are alone as much as I am, that happens once in a while. Wait. I will fetch you something to drink and you'll soon be on your feet again."

Miss Shortbread disappeared into the small adjoining room. Conner appreciated Miss Shortbread's care, but he nevertheless considered it better to disappear as quickly as possible. So he stood up, suffering the torments of hell, and crept out as quietly as he could.

He was met by an ice cold wind which made his head clearer. On his way out of the town he used every cover and reached the beach unnoticed. There he had time to examine himself. He looked as if he had bathed in chocolate. How on earth would he ever get clean again? Because if he turned up in front of Caitlin like this ...

Disheartened, he sat down in the sand. He pondered for a while and then gave up. Stretching out on the sand, he fell asleep.

When he awoke, it was already dark again. He had not been discovered, because it had rained all day. His fleece was certainly soaking wet and full of sand but there had also been some benefit from lying there all day and rolling back and forth. It had made him somewhat cleaner.

He was already expected at the byre. Caitlin drew him into her arms.

"I was extremely worried when you were not there this morning," she said. "I had forgotten what day it was and only noticed that we had a full moon after you were gone. I thought that you would not return," and added, after a sigh, "just like your father."

"Mum, I am sorry that you were worried. But you should not be. After all, I am back. And furthermore, I'll soon have the moon sickness under control," Conner boasted. "I have already outwitted the moon once."

"Honestly?" Caitlin asked in disbelief.

"Yes. I learn more about it every time." Conner was not completely at ease with what he said. But he would find out how he had been able to master the moon. Perhaps Abbie could help him to do so, if he told her the whole story.

"It would be a true blessing if you could overcome the moon sickness," Caitlin rejoiced. Then she teased, "Let's go inside so your girlfriend does not have to worry any longer."

Conner blushed, but it could not be seen in the dark byre.

Christmas And New Years Eve

On the following day, Adam visited his animals. He brought them four bales of the best hay in his pickup truck. As he entered the byre, he shouted exuberantly, "Merry Christmas to all of you! And I have one more gift for you." He quickly carried in a sack of dried sugar beet chips, which he tipped into two troughs. The sheep enthusiastically fell upon the treat. A grateful bah sounded here and there, but the gobbling was reward enough for Adam. He made sure that everything in the byre was just right and drove home.

After his candy orgy, Conner was not too crazy about the sugar beet chips and watched with amusement how greedily they all ate. Abbie looked especially cute. Several chips were caught in her honey-blonde little curls and she glowed like a living Christmas tree. As if she sensed that she was being watched, Abbie suddenly raised her head and looked at him. They both turned pink and instantly looked elsewhere. Ben had seen this and smirked around. Conner sauntered very casually over to Abbie, but when he stood beside her the nonchalance was gone.

On the contrary, he felt only a warm, loving feeling for Abbie.

"We are making a pleasant outing this evening. I'll show you Ullapool. You will like it. Especially now at Christmas, the whole little town is spruced up. And practically no humans walk around when it's late. We can really enjoy it."

"But the moon sickness," Abbie objected.

"Don't worry. We already have a waning moon. So there is no danger," Conner assured her. "So you're coming, okay?"

Abbie simply said, "Yes." and looked deep into his eyes for a brief moment.

"Agreed," Conner confirmed.

All day long, the sheep where unusually talkative, indeed, almost in high spirits. And as the sun set, Nathan and Ross distributed the last reserve of moorland mead. Ellie, Olivia, Caitlin and Megan lined up and sang the old ballad of Kieran and Heather. Holly and Daniel played their bagpipes between the verses. It was a truly festive evening. At a late hour, they all lay down contentedly to sleep.

That was the signal for Abbie and Conner. They crept quietly between the sleepers and out into the open. The sky appeared in holiday robes of dark blue, dotted with stars and a thick crescent moon for a brooch.

On the way into the little town, Conner told of his last full moon outings. With Abbie, he tried to find the difference between the uncontrollable and self-induced bleating attacks. The sole deviation in this case was Conner's earlier candy orgy. They decided to test this assumption at the next full moon. Abbie was fired up about helping him.

In the meantime, the couple had reached the harbor street. Conner played the tour guide.

"If you would please look to the right, you can see the fishing fleet of the brave Ullapool fishermen. Just ahead of us lies the market hall and directly opposite, the unrivaled Hotel Celtic."

Abbie giggled.

"May I now show you the famous Shopping Mile?" Conner asked gallantly.

Abbie snorted with laughter. She nodded in agreement. They crossed the roadway and strolled past the shop windows. The different displays were duly admired and commented on. They then reached Miss Shortbread's candy shop. Conner showed Abbie all the delicious things that he had got to know.

Arriving at the end of the row of houses, they turned into a residential area. Warm light and soft music came from many windows. Abbie suddenly stopped in front of a brick house with low windows.

"Come on. Let's get closer. I would like to know what it looks like inside," she said. Conner signaled for her to remain silent and crept ahead.

There were no humans in the room, but what splendor! Abbie pressed just as close as she could against the window. A richly decorated fir tree that immersed the room in a pleasant half-light from its Christmas lights attracted her gaze. The Christmas tree was decorated with countless red balls and golden ribbons. Chains with red and golden pearls were wrapped around it and a golden star showed off at the top. Lovingly wrapped, large and small packages were stacked under the tree. Abbie sighed and pulled Conner to the next house, then the next, further and further, until they reached the last house in the street. Abbie could not pull herself away from these windows. In Abbie's eyes, Conner discovered the same longing that he felt when the moon was full.

"Wait here for a moment. I'll be right back," Conner said and ran to the rear entrance. He squeezed through a small, partly open window and fell abruptly into the room. He stood still for a moment so his eyes could become accustomed to the darkness. Then he crept cautiously through the hall and into the living room. He took a glistening starlet garland from the tree and waved cheerfully to Abbie.

A moment later a storm of noise broke over

him; threatening growling followed by deafening barking. A giant Newfoundland dog crowded Conner into the corner of the room.

"Please be quiet, otherwise you'll wake up the whole street," Conner pleaded. "I only wanted a Christmas present for my girlfriend. But I can easily leave again. You just need to let me past."

The Newfoundland stopped barking. "Get out of here," he hissed. "No gift and make it snappy," he added emphatically.

The dog stepped aside. Conner still held the starlet chain in his hand when human voices and banging reached him from the stairway. He took a run-up, lowered his head and leaped through the window. The pane shattered with an enormous bang.

Abbie stood as if petrified, but Conner pushed her to the side of the garden. "Run as fast as you can. We'll meet at the beach," Conner shouted and ran into the street. He looked back once more for Abbie, but she had already disappeared into the gardens.

Luckily, the Newfoundland was called back by his master after a few yards. Since no one knew who the burglar had been, it seemed too dangerous to allow the dog to run free. By the time the homeowner had dressed and was ready to resume the pursuit, Conner had long since left the town behind him.

Abbie awaited him on the beach. Both of them were flushed and out of breath. Happy about their successful escape, they fell into each other's arms. Abbie cheered as Conner placed the hard-won chain around her.

She kissed him. He kissed her. They kissed each other. And then happened, what happens, when you are in love.

Epilogue

Conner and Abbie remained a happy couple. They loved each other and argued, tested their limits and each other and attempted to solve the mystery of moon sickness. They continued to move through the streets of Bettyhill and Ullapool at night and Conner indulged in his candy orgies, although somewhat more cautiously and with less incidental damage. He almost had his moonlight bleating under control and the citizens of both little towns began to make sense of it and the various break-ins. Miss Shortbread developed into a real specialist, although, as so often, it took a long time before the truth was accepted. By then it became a permanent part of horror and fireside stories.

In the following spring, a sweet baby lamb saw the light of the world on the night of the first full moon. Conner and Abbie named him Ryan Conner MacSheep.

His legs were still shaking when he bleated for the first time. But small fires of curiosity and zest for life already sparkled in his green eyes ...

To eliminate any uncertainty: Rams are male sheep, the female animals are called ewes and lamb is the designation for young and very young male and female sheep.

MacAngus Flock Cast

Conner MacSheep	ram, hero of the story
Abbie	young ewe, Conner's girlfriend
Caitlin MacAngus	Conner's loving mother, an ewe with a zest for life and bagpipe player
Conner MacSheep, Sr.	ram, Conner's missing father, about whom the wildest rumors circulate
Nathan MacAngus	oldest and wisest ram in the MacAngus flock, therefore Clan Chief; has an excellent memory

Ellie	middle-aged ewe, adorable and greedy, Olivia's sister
Olivia	spinster ewe with a propensity for gloomy prophecies
Janet	unassuming ewe with a desire for attention
Holly	ewe, Abbie's mother and Caitlin's friend, plays bagpipes
Ben	ram, friend of Conner and same age, Jamie's older brother
Jamie	lively young lamb, big fan of Conner and the Highland Sheep Games
Megan and Ross	parents of Ben and Jamie, friends of Caitlin and irreplaceable first aid team

Participants in the friendly Flock from the Grampian Mountains

John McMullen   oldest ram and
                      the flock's Clan Chief;
                      enjoys the annual
                      Highland Sheep Games

Jack Cross   ram in the prime of life,
                      contestant and musician

Hamish   ram, somewhat older
                      than Conner,
                      with great strength and
                      even more ego

Cat Bluebell   ewe, highly regarded
                      musician and singer

Plus various anonymous sheep
in supporting roles

Conner's Full Moon Favorites

Even if you do not personally suffer from the 'moon sickness', the following recipes can help you through various hurdles.

Scottish Tablet

Ingredients

    500 g / 2 2/3 cups granulated sugar

    60 g / 2 oz. butter

    3 ½ tablespoons condensed milk

    170 ml / 5 ¾ oz. water

Here's what to do: Place all ingredients in a large saucepan and heat gently unit the butter melts and the sugar is dissolved. Bring the mixture to a boil. Important: Stir constantly, because the mixture burns easily.

Now reduce the heat and simmer the mixture for approximately 10 minutes. It should now be thick, with the color of caramel.

Remove the pan from the heat and continue stirring for 5 minutes, while the mixture thickens. Before it solidifies, spread it onto an oiled baking tray, using a wooden spoon. You will now see the mixture harden very quickly.

Cut into bite-sized squares and allow to cool and harden for a further 5 minutes.

Store the completed Scottish tablet in an airtight container.

Tip: It also tastes excellent lukewarm!

Cranachan

Ingredients:

>300 g / 1 ½ cups fresh raspberries, frozen if necessary
>
>280 ml / 9 ½ oz. double cream or mascarpone
>
>2 tablespoons liquid honey
>
>2 tablespoons single malt whisky
>
>2 - 3 tablespoons oatmeal/rolled oats

Here's what to do: Roast the rolled oats dry in a heavy pan until golden-brown (10-20 minutes). Stir from time to time. Then allow the pan to cool. Whip the double cream in a bowl with a whisk until fairly stiff. Add the honey and whisky and continue whipping until the consistency is soft and creamy.

Place alternate layers of raspberries and cream in a clear stemmed glass and sprinkle roasted rolled oatmeal over the cream. Decorate with a raspberry. Place the dessert in a refrigerator for several hours or overnight.

Tip: Substitute strawberries for raspberries or mix the berries into the cream and freeze. A cool frozen delight!

Chocolate cake

Ingredients:

- 250 g / 1 1/8 cup butter
- 180 g / ¾ cup sugar
- 4 eggs
- 150 g / 5 oz. ground almonds or hazelnuts
- 250 g / 2 1/8 cup plain flour
- 6 teaspoons of dark cocoa powder
- 2 ½ teaspoons backing powder
- 100 g / 4 oz chocolate chips or chopped dark chocolate
- 150 g / 6 oz. chocolate frosting

Here's what to do: Beat butter, sugar and eggs until frothy. Add flour, baking powder and cocoa and mix thoroughly until mixture is uniform.

Finally, fold in ground almonds and chocolate chips by hand.

Place the dough in an oiled springform pan, smooth the surface and bake for 45-50 minutes at 190° C / 345° F.

Carefully remove the springform wall after

baking. Allow the cake to cool to body temperature and cover with frosting. It tastes best on the day after baking.

Tip: Enjoy the cake with whipped cream or vanilla sauce.

Shortbread

Even if Miss Shortbread is not among the main characters in this story, she deserves mention as a delicious biscuit.

Ingredients:

    200 g / 1 cup butter

    85 g / ¾ cup superfine sugar

    175 g / 1 ½ cup flour

    60 g / ½ cup rice flour or cornstarch

    1 tablespoon sugar for decoration

Here's what to do: Preheat oven to 150°C / 300° F. Oil a backing sheet and cover with baking paper. Mix butter and sugar with hand mixer until foamy. Add the sieved flour and mix to a soft dough. Briefly knead on a surface dusted with flour and form into a ball. Roll out to form a circle, a good 1/2`` thick. Place on baking paper and score 12 portions with a sharp knife. Bake for 30-40 minutes, until golden brown. Sprinkle with sugar and cut or break along the scored lines while hot. You can enjoy shortbread hot or cold.

*Whisky truffle*s

Ingredients:

> 450 g / 16 oz. high quality dark chocolate, broken into pieces, half of the chocolate will be required for the coating
>
> 3 tablespoons cream
>
> 3 tablespoons of your favorite whisky

Here's what to do: Melt half of the chocolate in a double boiler. Add cream and whisky and stir until completely mixed. Allow mixture to cool to room temperature.

Scoop thumb-sized portions, place on non-stick paper, and chill until mixture hardens completely. Now form small balls and place them in the refrigerator until hard.

Meanwhile, melt the remaining chocolate for the covering in the double boiler. Using a dipping fork, dip the cold balls in the liquid chocolate and allow to cool on non-stick paper.

Warning: Close all doors and windows when you eat these truffles, especially on full moon nights!

Whisky honey

The easiest way to have something absolutely delicious and versatile in the pantry.

Ingredients:
>500 g / 16 oz. thick, creamy honey (e.g. rapeseed honey)
>
>3 tablespoons whisky, preferably Scottish single malt with a strong flavor.

Here's what to do: Gently heat the honey in a double boiler. Stir in the whisky and allow the mixture to cool. Store in an airtight jar.

Use it as the Scots do, to sweeten your tea or porridge. It also tastes marvelous on a buttered roll.

Tip: If you cannot get to sleep, make yourself some warm milk or hot chocolate and stir in some whisky honey. You'll see. It really works!

If you still don't fall asleep immediately, you at least had a delicious nightcap!

Special thanks to my husband and daughter for their advice, help and proofreading during this project. I also wish to thank all the kind people who supported and advised me in the course of my first "big" book.

On to the next opus!

You can find news about Conner and his friends at:

    www.edition-schoene-buecher.de

.